Jubilee House Prayers, Poems and Promises

Honor and Recognize the Sacrifice and Service of Women Veterans

Jubilee House Prayers, Poems and Promises:

Inspiration for Homeless Women Veterans

by

Barbara Summey Marshall

Maya Valrissa Louise Marshall

Copyright @ 2017 by Barbara Summey Marshall and Maya Valrissa Louise Marshall

All rights reserved. No part of this publication may be reproduced, distributed or transmitted in any form or by any means, without prior written permission.

Resurrection Veterans Ministry Services

P. O. 9634

Fayetteville, N.C. 28311

Jubilee House Prayers, Poems

And Promises: Inspiration for Homeless Women Veterans ISBN-13: 978 – 0692854808

ISBN-10: 0692854800

Stock photos taken from the web are credited as such.

We dedicate this book of inspiration and hope

To my paternal grandmother, **Earn Lou Whiteside**, who loved me with her whole heart and wanted to see me go to college, and to my Mother, **Louise Syprus Summey**, a Woman who

Needed a little Jubilee and to my husband

James Cornelius Neely, Jr. a Vietnam Era, Semper Fi, US Marine

Who helped to prepare the Jubilee House for Homeless women Veterans.

Although deceased, these people live on in our hearts.

Hermeneutics

The Jubilee House Prayers, Poems and Promises is a book born out of a decade plus of offering spiritual support, transitional housing and timely assistance to Sister Veterans who have faced homelessness. This book is historical, spiritual and longitudinal.

The writers of the book are women veterans with varied experiences. Barbara Summey Marshall is a a former Navy Chaplain, Womanist Theologue and Social Activist. Maya Valrissa Louise Marshall is a Combat Veteran of the Afghanistan war who has faced the dangers of being deployed in a war zone. Maya is also a fulltime student and aspiring employee in the health profession who is battling to return to a life of productivity and overcome the trauma of war. Both women are disabled veterans who are committed to assisting other women veterans who are seeking to make a fresh start. This book of prayers, poems and promises are reflective of the daily challenges that may occur in the life of homeless women veterans.

Many women veterans have faced Military Sexual Trauma (MST), rape and sexual harassment during their time of military services. For some women recovering from the trauma of sexual assault has negatively impacted their ability to get back on their feet, make a fresh start and begin a new life after homelessness.

Some women are still unpacking the inhumane experience and dealing with the residuals of low self esteem and disorientation. For some the lack of acknowledgement by the military community and the fact that women veterans have faced under reported sexual assault and rape has led to isolation and reintegration challenges.

This book is hopeful and motivational for transitional women veterans and their families. This book of poems and prayers are restorative and reflective. The book is written to honor and acknowledge the service and sacrifice of women veterans, many of whom are also disabled and have faced the complex experience of homelessness.

The authors of this book began opening their family home to homeless women veterans in March 2005. In August 2010, the women veterans purchased a Department of Veterans Affairs Foreclosure in Fort Bragg/Fayetteville NC to help and to house homeless women veterans and their children. The women veterans named the sanctuary the Jubilee

House named after the Leviticus 25 reference to the Year of Jubilee or the year of Refreshing.

In January of 2011, the American Broadcasting Companies Inc. network reached out to the women veterans and discussed the possibility of renovating the 1300 square feet VA Foreclosure purchased by the women veterans. After much dialogue, prayer and consideration Barbara Summey Marshall and James Cornelius Neely Jr.(now deceased) along with Maya Valrissa Louise Marshall and C. Roberto Clemente Marshall consented to have the ABC Extreme Makeover team rebuild the original Jubilee House. James was a United States Marine veteran who served during the Vietnam War and suffered the effects of agent orange and Post Traumatic Stress Disorder. James Cornelius Neely Jr. died March 2011 amid the strenuous, emotional interviews conducted by the American Broadcasting Companies Inc. producers.

The offer by American Broadcasting Companies Incorporated to rebuild the forlorn Jubilee House seemed like the answer to our prayers and hopes for honoring women veteran. ABC sought to honor the service and sacrifices of women veterans in a manner that was historical, unorthodox and avant garde. American Broadcasting Companies Inc. acknowledged the presence of a population of veterans that had essentially been "invisible" and discounted.

Moreover, the September 2011 episode announced to the world that women veterans are to be recognized for their service and sacrifice and are worthy of a nationally televised Extreme Makeover House rebuilt in their honor. We was overjoyed to have former First Lady

Michelle Robinson Obama and Ty Pennington present for the week of rebuilding.

Sadly for the years following the rebuild or renovation of the Jubilee House in July 2011, the attempts have been numerous to turn back the clock and pretend that women veterans are still invisible. There have been many failed attempts to make us fearful and to distract us from the ministry of reaching out to homeless women veterans. Many military communities like Fort Bragg/Fayetteville, North Carolina are plagued with deeply rooted and dangerous misogynist patterns. The preponderance of hatred is even more perverse when cultural demographics of race and disability become factors.

The fact that the Jubilee House was purchased and started by Black women veterans was not been accepted or welcomed. This was evidenced by the staggering degree of hostility, hatred and violence toward the Black women veterans who started the ministry of helping homeless women veterans.

Nonetheless, before and after the rebuild of the Jubilee House in July 2011, the ministry to women veterans has been an odyssey of transformation. We have witnessed the forward movement of more than 2500 contacts with women veterans which includes their families and children. Many of thes military families have a million valid reasons to lose hope and however some reasons are manufactured by those who are indifferent to the service and sacrifice of women veterans. We have seen women veterans seek recovery services, regain the custody of children, purchase and maintain automobiles, accept employment, move beyond prostitution and make a fresh start. We are blessed to have seen such miracles.

The real mission/ministry of the Jubilee House for Women veteran is how women veterans residents, volunteers and others were able to stay the course while being undermined, investigated, discredited and taunted by local and state entities. Sometimes the Jubilee House felt a shelter in the midst of the storm. We felt like the Hebrew children in Exodus

Chapter 14 :13 – 14

13 But Moses said to the people, Do not Be afraid, stand firm, and see the Deliverance that the Lord will Accomplish for you today; for the Egyptians whom you see today you Shall never see again. 14. The Lord will Fight for you, and you have only to keep Still." (New Revised Standard Version)

– "We had to stand still and see that even though we were surrounded by that mean ol' Pharaoh and his army, there was still many reasons to be hopeful. There was walls of criticism and condemnation from local homeless veterans providers, but there was hope and restoration within our gates as we believed that the God of Jubilee would see us through.

Women Veterans are deserving of Prayers, Poems, and Promises. Over 3 Million have served since the beginning of history. Some had to disguise their gender and others like Frances Clayton disguised herself as Frances Clalin to fight in the Civil War. During the battle, the Union army found a dead woman wearing a uniform of a Confederate private. Jennie Hodgers, also known as Albert Cashier of the 95the Illinois Infantry and Loreta Janeta Valazquez served the Confederacy as spy Lieutenant Harry Buford. Many women were wounded in battle, and some women died but many were determined to fight for freedom. We salute these brave women.

Contents

Introduction..21

A Prayer for Homeless Sisters...23

They Said – A Poem for My Homeless Sisters...25

A Promise For Homeless Sisters...27

Prayer for Justice and Equality... 30

Prayers for Incarcerated Women Veterans......33

A Community of Silence..36

Prayers of Protection for Women Veterans... 40

Watching and Waiting...43

Experience Jubilee...45

Invisible Veterans………………………………..…..49

Sisters We Served….……………………………....…..53

When the Hate is Great, the Hope is Greater………………………………….. ..56

Get In Formation……………………………… 63

The Passing Shadow of Homelessness…………………………..… 65

Invisible War against Invisible Women Veterans…………………………….68

Sister Veterans Make Lemonade…………….. 73

Why We Must Fight Back……………………………..…..…..78

Just Like That……………………………….....……..80

About to Rise Up………………………………,………. ….83

Introduction

Stock Photo. Courtesy of Military Files

Jubilee – Time of Refreshing

The Book of Leviticus from Hebrew Scriptures is pre-eminently a book of worship and thanksgiving. This book paints a picture of The Year of Jubilee. Jubilee was in many measures a time of economic and spiritual restoration for a people who have been in the heat of battle. Leviticus 25: 1- 55 reminds us that though the Hebrew community was weary and waxing tired from the wilderness journey, that the Holy God has sojourned with them throughout this historical pilgrimage.

Likewise, this book of prayers, poems and promises offers words of consolation and hope to homeless, marginalized and frequently invisible women veterans. We are not forgotten. We are not unrecognized. America will someday clearly acknowledge and honor the service and sacrifice of the daughters of this nation. So my Sister Veterans be encouraged, be steadfast and continue to live in peace and happiness.

A Prayer for Homeless Sisters

We offer this prayer for your peace of mind and safety.

My Sister Veteran we see the road that you have traveled...

The long nights and the difficult days.

The times of solitude and silence

When far from family and friends

The times of worry and distress when even your best

Didn't seem good enough

But you kept the faith and believed against all odds

That dreaming and holding on was the way to go

Keep on keeping on my Sister

For God is Listening to Every Word

God sees your distress and difficulty

God will see you through.

Barbara Summey Marshall, NSWC, Oct. 1996

A Poem for You My Homeless Sisters

They Said

They Wrote

They thought

They Hoped

They could not see your worth

They presumed

They listened

They assumed

They ignored

They did not see your value

They waited

They rehearsed

They could not rewrite

Your Story, Your Courage, Your destiny

They could not rewrite history

My Sister you are history in the re-writing…

Former First Lady Michelle Obama and Ty Pennington –honoring women veterans with their presence at Jubilee House Reveal after ABC Extreme HomeMakeover in Fayetteville, NC .July 2011.

A Promise For You My Homeless Sisters

Our promise to you My Sisters

Is to see your worth

To value your service

To honor your sacrifice

To acknowledge the legacy of faith

Our promise to you

My Sister is to see beyond your challenges

And earthly losses

To remind you of your possibilities

And capabilities

Our promise to you

My Sister is to wait with you as the

Storm is passing

Through your life

To offer consolation and an umbrella of hope.

Our promise to you my Sister is to cheer you

On as you make a new beginning,

Releasing the pain,

Ignoring the naysayers and haters.

Our promise to you My Sister

Is to believe in you and

Value your service.

Original Jubilee House purchased Aug. 2010

Prayer for Justice and Equality

Let justice roll down like waters and righteousness like a mighty stream

Let the mountains lift up their voices and make a loud noise that transcends our tears

We cry out for Transgender Justice, Civil Rights Justice, Equal Rights Justice, Gay Rights Justice, Human Rights Justice, Black Lives Matter, Latino Lives Matter and Gender Justice, Older Peoples Justice, Disabled Peoples Justice

We cry aloud as women veterans of all eras, conflicts, wars and scrimmages.

Let justice roll down like waters and

Righteousness like a mighty stream.

We resist invisibility, we resist hatred,

We resist intimidation, we resist lynching,

We resist crucifixion, we resist homelessness.

We stand for courage. We stand for resilience

We stand for determination.

We stand for longevity. We stand for life.

Let justice roll down like waters and

Righteousness like a mighty stream.

We stand for safe spaces for women veterans to serve this nation without fear of sexual assault and harassment.

We stand for discharges that will reflect our service and will not be weaponized to keep us silent. We stand for promotion and advancement.

We stand for ranks that are regal and righteous.

We stand for Justice and Equalitty

Nicole Heffel, Navy Veteran and Attorney began mentoring program to help incarcerated women veterans in California.

Prayers for Incarcerated Women Veterans

She's Worth It.

The mentoring program started by a Navy veteran to reach incarcerated women veterans.

She is a former master at arms, Navy Police Officer who wanted to help.

The weekly support group was just what was needed to show concern for those forgotten.

To reach these women who had deployed to

Persian Gulf, Iraq, Afghanistan to fight for freedom.

She's Worth It.

Twenty female veteran inmates have come through this circle of change.

Rebooting lives and awakening hope

Nicole Heffel organized the outreach.

More Justice programs are needed for the justice involved women veterans.

Justice involved Women have different unique challenges – higher incidences of physical and family abuse. Sexual assault and military trauma.

They are more likely to be exposed to violence and have mental health diagnoses.

These Sisters are our Sisters.

She's Worth It.

So Prayers we are offering as the incarceration rate for women veterans is growing

State and federal prisons are harbingers for transformation.

These Sister Veterans are ready for intensive counseling and reintegration training.

She's Worth It.

In Your Mercy hear our prayers

Residents of Jubilee House, 2015.

A Community of Silence

No Voices, no words.

No Letters, no support

But still the dreams lives on.

No Articles, No recognition

No Invitation, No Gratitude

But Still the dream lives on

Did anyone think it

Preposterous that women veterans

Who bought houses to honor veterans

Pitches in benefits

But do not live in the house

She kept it afloat

Little donations came in

She gave her all.

No gratitude. No acknowledgement.

No Honor. No recognition.

But criticism, ostracism,

Death threats, Harm and malice

Hate from the State

Local animosity and conspiracies

The People of faith are watching

Them bury us with myths and accusations

Who stood with Jesus

Who went to the tomb

Courageous women when dared to dream

A Community of Silence will Speak

Our Holocaust and wish they had

Done more than pray.

We are the least of these, the forgotten,

The invisible. The marginalized.

We are the seeds of tomorrow.

We will blossom forth and chains will fall.

We will dance the dreams of Lavena Johnson, India Kager, Marianna Rollins, Danyelle Tucker, LaKeina Monique Francis, Ashley White, Iris Armstrong, Pamela Donovan, Morganne McBeth, Laura Walker, Emily Perez, Janelle King, Jennifer Moreno…..

And Jalisha VonshayTucker.

We will not be a Community of Silence

Prayers of Protection for Women Veterans

Eternal God who is Mother and Father

We ask your protection of women veterans

Protection from hurt, harm and danger

Protection from disease, distress and despair

Protection from domestic violence, military sexual assault, rape and emotional harassment

Eternal God who is Mother and Father

We ask your protection of women veteran

Protection from hostility, hatred, and hinderance

Protection from invisibility, implausibility and incredulity

Protection from violence, vicious rumors and viral false accusations

Eternal God who is Mother and Father

We humbly ask your protection of women veterans.

Watching and Waiting

This Dream that we have

Has us Watching and Waiting

Responding to calls for help from Sisters who

Are in harms way.

We made an effort to lift those with

Heavy burdens, to offer Jubilee.

A time of Refreshing

A moment of rest and sanctuary

To be safe with Sisters who have served.

Watching and Waiting

Some are far from hope and healing

Many are invisible and forgotten

Not welcomed in community

But we are watching and waiting

With soup and crackers

Fresh towels and wash clothes

Mercy and Spiritual Formation

Referrals for treatment

Acknowledgment of their service

Watching and Waiting.

ABC Renovated Jubilee House, Sept. 2011

Experience Jubilee

A Place to call home.

A place that is safe.

No tricks to turn or sexual favors are due

Experience Jubilee

The sheets are clean and the pillows are soft.

We offer to pray and mention your name

My Sister your life is our mission

Your recovery is our ministry

We purchased a house to bring you home

Experience Jubilee

The house needed work and repairs

But we lived as a family

Made meals and sat together and talked

Cynthia Humphrey and Doris McDaniel were eager to serve

Many Sisters like Linda Ellerbe came with words of hope and home cooked meals.

Experience Jubilee

Luvonne Holloway and Jessica Dade took time to care and offer spiritual support

Some women veterans were hurt and limping with cares.

Many joined in the refrain that we can help ourselves

Experience Jubilee

Others brought harm and danger not understanding

Their worth and value

Some women veterans were used as pawn to sow discard and unrest

Others were so accustomed to disruption that into house came their pain and pandemonium

Experience Jubilee

Others battled with issues that were life long burdens but we cared and hung on their with them

Some victims of domestic violence were fearful that the partner would find them and end their lives

Some women veterans just needed a respite from the litany of discouragement

Experience Jubilee

Priscilla Patrick and Natalie Carter gave of their time and managed the homes with compassion

Some women veterans tried to bring into the house the habits that were weighing them down

Some were simply ready to make a better life and release the old refrain

Some women veterans were nurturing children and guiding their lives

Experience Jubilee

Some women were already employed but lacking transportation had to struggle

Some women veterans came walking the tightrope of tumult and tribulation

Some women veterans took what was given and wanted to be a blessing to others

Experience Jubilee

A time of refreshing.

Stock Photo Courtesy of Military Files

Invisible Veterans

WAACS, WAVES, WASPS, SPARS

We don't see you.

You fly planes, nurse the wounded,

Soldier on, Organize mail, Fight Battles

Pray for the Weary.

Bandage the broken

Encourage the faltering

We don't see you.

You went to battle

But must fight to be buried at Arlington National Cemetery

WWII WASP Elaine Harmon

 fought to be laid to

Rest with her fellow veterans

You blessed our souls

With prayers and sermons

You operate missiles

And dodge bullets and incoming mortar rounds.

We don't see you.

We make you invisble.

You died in the line of duty

You died on ship, shore and in the air

We don't want to see you.

You are invisible.

But we see ourselves.

Former President Obama honors WASP for courage and dedication. File photo.

Maya Valrissa Marshall's Unit to Afghanistan- 359 Scandevils, Fort Eustis, Virginia 2012.

Sisters We Served

Sisters we served

From ship to shore

From Fort Campbell to Fort Hood

Sisters we served

From battlefield to bunkers

Sisters we served

From chapels to hospitals

From Camp Lejeune to Virginia Beach

Sisters we served

From Cold weather training to Desert military Installations

Sisters we served

From standing the watch to keeping the peace

From Vietnam to Afghanistan

From Persian Gulf to Iraq

From dangerous missions to hometown hostility

Sisters we served

From Navy Seals to Special Operations Command

From villages in the Middle East to Ships in Blue Water

From USS Carl Vision to Fort Belvoir

Sisters we served.

File photo. Courtesy of Military Files.

Where Hate is Great, Hope is Greater

We faced Hate when we enlisted and went to boot camp

We faced the doubts and the sabotage as

We signed our names on the dotted line

We raised our right hand and swore to defend

We faced Hate from the Commanders and Colonels and Chiefs.

We wondered why the way was so tumultuous

Where Hate is Great, Hope is Greater.

When we bought the leaky house to help homeless women

Veterans it seemed so absurd and destined for fail

But we housed six homeless veterans and four children

And offered meals and a place to heal.

We faced hate when ABC called our number and offered to come

Pitch in to Honor Women veterans.

The Death threats, Hostility, Myths and Jealousy stood like

Soldiers on our steps.

The Hate filled the parking lot with cars that shined lights at our porch

To scare us and make us know that we have reasons to worry

We faced Hate when the media printed half truths and endangered our lives

The paper Said that we moved into the Housing for homeless veterans.

The State tried to get the volunteers to support the myth,

We faced Hate when the State took us to court for refusing to

Surrender the name of homeless women veterans.

We faced Hate when they

Threw us in jail without our medication

We faced hate when they plotted and conspired to find something to use against disabled women veterans trying to do a good

We faced hate when they hired private investigators to follow us night and

Day.

We faced hate when the Deposition was demanded

But nothing that we said was different from what we had done to help homeless women veterans

Heather Black was bitter and angry because of the ABC Jubilee House renovation

She tried to poison the veteran residents against us and pledged to do her best to bring us down

She was enraged and filled with the fire of hatred against us

She tried every angle to destroy and discredit disabled women veterans

The Sec of State affirmed her merciless measures as though spite and hostility was legal because were a charitable ministry

We faced hate from Local people. State, City, homeless advocates all because of the Jubilee House

We faced hate when the unknown calls said leave or be harmed

We faced hate when our garage door was kicked in and the police

Would not come and help.

We faced hate alone when ABC went silent and spoke not a word.

We faced hate when the criticism came from all directions determined to

Bring up down.

We faced hate when the State turned a blind eyes as paid staff pounded

 Disabled women veterans

We faced hate when the lawyer was malevolent and the volunteers

were pallbearers.

We faced hate when the rules were changed to insure our unjust treatment.

But we sought Spiritual Strength

With a Song for the night Season.

Jesus is my portion, a constant friend is he,

His eye is on the sparrow

I know He watching me

We Sought the Jubilee of God who Illuminated our way.

We Fought for Justice and Honor for Women Veterans.

We filed a federal complaint and asked for a security detail

Then We stood still and waited on God.

Where Hate is Great, Hope is Greater.

Women Veterans military sorority volunteers.

Get in Formation

Prayers for you Woman Veteran

Who think that life is too hard to bear

Who look at struggle as lingering clouds

Who think of difficulties as lasting raindrops

Who remember days when all was well and good.

Prayers for you who has worn the uniform

Spoken the oath, been to basic training and

Who must now return to a life of dreaming and believing

We prayed for you woman veteran

And hope that you would see your strength.

You are greater than your current situation

More powerful than your greatest weakness

Mightier than that habit or inclination

Arise Woman veteran take your place in formation.

Jubilee House Volunteers and Former Program Participants.

The Passing Shadow of Homelessness

They came to Jubilee House jaded, wishing for other options

Other possibilities, Other answers

They come to us angry, grieving, wondering what lead to homelessness.

They come to us thinking that there must be a mistake, an error.

Someone forgot to make a deposit in their dream account

They came to us wishing for better days,

Quick turn arounds, and early solutions.

They come to us hoping that the reality for homelessness will be

Like a passing shadow over

Homelessness is a Passing Shadow

Homelessness is new for some

And very familiar for others

Homelessness is a cave, a hiding place where shadows cover your dreams

Homelessness is comfortable for some,

A Long term companion.

Homelessness is where you hide

From dreams and responsibilities

Homelessness is where you hide from

Disappointment and Embarrassment

Homelessness is where the dormant can sleep and the uncertain can languish

Homelessness is a thinking pattern a mindset, a whimsical

Detour from pain and disappointment

Homelessness is an unwelcomed state of being without a home.

File photo. Courtesy of Military stock.

Invisible War Against Invisible Women Veterans

There is an Invisible War Against Invisible Women Veterans

These women are Soldiers, Sailors, Air Force personnel, Marines and Coast Guard.

These women have been raped and abused,
Sexually assaulted and discredited.

Many use their voices to help other women like BriGette McCoy, Diana Danis, Ruth Marie Donaldson, Jas Boothe, Tee Marie and Regina Vasquez

Some women have been sanctioned, silenced and maligned.

Other women veterans have been murdered and maimed like Lavena Johnson, India Kager and Jalisha Vonshay Tucker.

There is an Invisible War against Invisible Women.

These women have unmerited adverse Discharges and challenges for life.

These women have no access to medical care at VA Medical Facilities

These women have served as Chaplains, unit Commanders, cooks, nurses, and

Truck drivers.

These women have deployed to Persian Gulf, Iraq and Afghanistan.

These women have faced the enemy in the barracks and on the streets of America.

These women are homeless and hoping that America still cares.

These women have advocates like Pam Campos-Palma, Cynthia Humhrey, Jaretha Marbury, Linda Ellerbe, Doris McDaniel and Natalie Carter.

These women are Mothers, Sisters, Daughters, Nieces and Spouses.

There is an Invisible War Against Invisible Women Veterans…

But it won't succeed..

Sgt Donna R. Johnson of Raeford N.C. and wife Sgt Tracy Dice Johnson. Donna's wife received survivor benefits following her death in Afghanistan in 2012.

File photo . Courtesy of www.

Woman Veteran Chef made mesls for the residents.

Sister Veterans make Lemonade

Sisters make lemonade

Life has been harsh and difficult to manage

The valleys have been low and the mountains high

Sisters Make Lemonade.

Beyonce taught us well and made it clear

That when life gives you lemons

Make lemonade.

Making lemonade can be as simple

Stepping back and taking a deep breath when overwhelmed.

Or applying for another job after four denials in a row.

Making lemonade is taking back from your life from drugs and pharmaceuticals

Improving your credit score and opening a small business

Refusing to be depressed and oppressed and suppressed any longer by people who do not recognize your worth

Refraining from any destructive life habits and patterns,

Make lemonade,

Building new relationships with family members and with children

Pausing to look in the mirror recognizing that the face in the mirror is someone who has value and purpose

Honoring your spirit and your mind by refusing known toxins and carcinogens,

Taking life one day at a time and refusing to be overwhelmed by that which can not be changed

Make lemonade

Refusing to be frightened by scare tactics and acts of intimidation

Calling out those who are not working to make you strong but to weaken your bodies and spirit

Make lemonade

Having a DD214 and still being treated like you are not a veteran because of your gender

Make Lemonade

Encourage yourself by recalling those things that you do well

Your many capabilities and possibilities and reliabilities

Know you better anyone else

Make lemonade

Your best days are ahead and the past is behind

Make lemonade.

Make lemonade

Proud Women Veterans Photo courtesy of the web.

Why We Must Fight Back

Spiritual fortitude helps on days when going

Forward is a voluminous task

Spiritual connection is water to the soil thirsty fingers

With doubt and disappointment

Spiritual acumen is boldness in the face of

Dire circumstance

Spiritual readiness is aligning the gear

Needed to bring back to life your spirit

Spiritual formation moving in sync with justice,

Using our voices, posting our concerns, filing a complaint for Justice.

Civil rights violations and negligence

We standing our ground

Resisting fear and intimidation,

Peace and hope.

Spiritual support is our gift to you.

Just Like That

We opened our doors with dollars from our pockets.

Pension and Disability Compensation came together

And dreamed that somehow we could

Find a VA Foreclosure that could become a home

For homeless women veterans.

Then Just Like That American Broadcasting Companies Inc.

Offered to make our house over

We agreed with reservation, but never met with the

Mayor or City Council. Seemed

Like a good idea they said to each other we never heard.

Then six months later the community crashed.

The winds got colder and the evil words printed on the front page news.

Just Like That.

We were serving homeless women veterans and sacrificing our time

To honor the daughters of our nation.

We was moving furniture and cooking meals. We was making

Calls and offering prayers.

We was seeing the invisible and listening to the lost.

Just Like That.

The Invisible women veterans did not matter once the Bus was moved.

Jubilee House Training Session. 2013

About to Rise Up..

We about to Rise up

We been down long enough

We about to Rise up

Your laws are not just

We about to Rise up

Your calculations were misconstrued

We about to Rise up

Nothing of this is new

We about to Rise Up

We have been through this before

We prayed and got Spiritual Support

To come through back then

We about to Rise up again

Women Veterans this is your

Resurrection and Your Rising

We Rising Up.

Luvonne Holloway and other Jubilee House volunteers pitching in with lawn beautification.

Dedicated to our Sister Veterans

Still I Rise

By Maya Angelou, Acclaimed Poet and Writer

You may write me down in history
With your bitter, twisted lies,
You may tread me in the very dirt
But still, like dust, I'll rise.

Does my sassiness upset you?
Why are you beset with gloom?
'Cause I walk like I've got oil wells
Pumping in my living room.

Just like moons and like suns,
With the certainty of tides,
Just like hopes springing high,
Still I'll rise.

Did you want to see me broken?
Bowed head and lowered eyes?
Shoulders falling down like teardrops.
Weakened by my soulful cries.

Does my haughtiness offend you?
Don't you take it awful hard
'Cause I laugh like I've got gold mines
Diggin' in my own back yard.

You may shoot me with your words,
You may cut me with your eyes,
You may kill me with your hatefulness,
But still, like air, I'll rise.

Does my sexiness upset you?
Does it come as a surprise
That I dance like I've got diamonds
At the meeting of my thighs?

Out of the huts of history's shame
I rise
Up from a past that's rooted in pain
I rise
I'm a black ocean, leaping and wide,
Welling and swelling I bear in the tide.
Leaving behind nights of terror and fear
I rise
Into a daybreak that's wondrously clear
I rise

Bringing the gifts that my ancestors gave,
I am the dream and the hope of the slave.
        I rise
        I rise
        I rise.

Maya Angelou

•

The Year of Jubilee

8 " 'Count off seven sabbath years—seven times seven years—so that the seven sabbath years amount to a period of forty-nine years.

9 Then have the trumpet sounded everywhere on the tenth day of the seventh month; on the Day of Atonement sound the trumpet throughout your land.

10 Consecrate the fiftieth year and proclaim liberty throughout the land to all its inhabitants. It shall be a jubilee for you; each of you is to return to your family property and to your own clan.

11 The fiftieth year shall be a jubilee for you; do not sow and do not reap what grows of itself or harvest the untended vines.

12 For it is a jubilee and is to be holy for you; eat only what is taken directly from the fields.

13 " 'In this the Year of Jubilee everyone is to return to their own property.

(Leviticus 25:8-13 New International Version of the Bible.)

Memorial Page
To
Honor All Fallen
Women
Veterans.

Faces of 1,000 Women Veterans Flag at the Jubilee
House, Fayetteville, North Carolina

About the Authors

Barbara Summey Marshall is a proud Navy Veteran. Womanist Theologue and Social Activist. She is Duke University Divinity School graduate and earned a Doctor of Ministry from United Theological Seminary. Proud Mom. Author. Lover of all things Outdoors especially the North Carolina mountains.

Maya Valrissa Louise Marshall is a proud US Army veteran. She completed a tour of Combat Duty in Afghanistan. She is a HBCU Student and avid Volunteer. She is actively seeking employment with the Department of Veterans Affairs. Maya enjoys extensive travel of the United States and around the globe. She treasures time spent with family and friends.

Acknowledgements

Deeply grateful for Jubilee Family, Friends, and Community who enhance this journey called life. The people near and dear are my siblings --Lucy Summey Greer, Susan Teneal Summey, Clarence Summey Jr. and the late Thomas Summey, Pearl Summey Dinnall, Clarence Johnny Summey and several others. We have weathered many storms together and lived through the times of Jubilee. We are also grateful for their spouses and children and grandchildren.

Deeply grateful to Maya Valrissa Louise Marshall, a Combat Veteran and consummate professional, and son, Clifton Roberto Clemente Thurgood Marshall III, who is as magnanimous as his name. Roberto has a heart for the homeless and hurting. He has kept the faith throughout this ABC renovation and painful ordeal that followed.

Deeply grateful for all 3 million plus women veterans who have fought for freedom. Thanks to all who pitched in as we stood the watch, traveled far away or just around the corner to our duty stations. You cared for our children, mowed our lawns and whispered prayers for our safety and peace of mind.

Deeply grateful for several good friends who waited us and prayed for us as we journeyed through the labyrinth of unprecedented opposition following the rebuild of the Jubilee House -- Paula Hutchison Johnson, Natalie Carter, Cynthia Humphrey, Dr. Valerie Fields, Rev. Dr. Deborah Kathleen Blanks, Rev. Donna Patterson, Rev. Carol Patterson and Luvonne Holloway.

Deeply grateful for all women veterans who have passed through the proving ground of homelessness and uncertainty on the way to stability and confidence, your journey is our marker. We have prayed for you and offered a place of sanctuary for you and your families.

Deeply grateful for all women veterans who have survived Military Sexual Trauma and reached back to insure that veterans understand this invisible war against our sister and brother veterans is a scourge against us all.

Deeply grateful for all volunteers, faith partners, silent supporters, well wishers, onlookers and friends who value the service and support of women veterans enough to help a "Sister when she is down." Many gave sacrificially of their time, energy, enthusiasm and resources.

Deeply grateful for Pastor Larry Gordon and First Sergeant Melanie Robinson Gordon and the Mount Hebrew African Methodist Episcopal Zion Church Family for beseeching God on our behalf. Thanks for pitching in and for conducting worship at the Jubilee House. We are glad *that "somebody prayed for us and had us on their minds…took the time and prayed for us."*

Finally, Deeply grateful to American Broadcasting Companies Inc. and affiliates for honoring the service and sacrifice of women veterans with a rebuilt "Jubilee House" and a flag with the faces of 1000 women veterans.

Also deeply grateful for the presence of former First Lady Michelle Robinson Obama and benevolent television personality, Ty Pennington. Both of these people are staunch supporters and strong advocates for

Women veterans and all members of the armed forces. We also grateful for the appearance of Rihanna – honoring women veterans. Their presence made the event mega- phenomenal. Wow!!

This *avant garde* act of recognizing women veterans was sacred. Whenever the legacy of the service and sacrifice of women veterans is shared, this historic act by American Broadcasting Companies Incorporated will be recorded as a part of that enduring legacy. The act of rebuilding the Jubilee House has cleared the way for even greater acts of honor and recognition for Women Veterans.

A Page for Your Jubilee Thoughts ....

www.ingramcontent.com/pod-product-compliance
Lightning Source LLC
Chambersburg PA
CBHW070313100426
42743CB00011B/2443